WINGS OF WAR

Bombers of World War II

by Nancy Robinson Masters

Content Review:

Research Department

United States Air Force Museum

CAPSTONE
HIGH/LOW BOOKS
an imprint of Capstone Press

C A P S T O N E   P R E S S

818 North Willow Street • Mankato, Minnesota 56001
http://www.capstone-press.com

Library of Congress Cataloging-in-Publication Data
Robinson Masters, Nancy.
    Bombers of World War II/by Nancy Robinson Masters.
        p. cm.--(Wings of war)
    Includes bibliographical references and index.
    Summary: Introduces the different kinds of bombers used during World War II, their capabilities, the kinds of missions on which they were sent, and any special characteristics.
ISBN 1-56065-532-1
        1. Bombers--United States--History--Juvenile literature. 2. World War, 1939-1945--Aerial operations, American. [1. Bombers. 2. Airplanes, Military. 3. World War, 1939-1945--Aerial operations.] I. Title. II. Title: Bombers of World War Two. III. Title: Bombers of World War 2. IV. Series: Wings of war (Mankato, Minn.)
UG1242.B6R63   1998
623.7'463'097309044--DC21

                                            97-5998
                                              CIP
                                               AC

The author would like to thank Harry Wadsworth, Laura Thaxton, and Bill Masters for their research assistance.

Editorial credits
Editor, Matt Doeden; cover design, Timothy Halldin; illustrations, James Franklin; photo research, Michelle L. Norstad

Photo credits
American Airpower Heritage Museum, 10, 38, 40
Archive Photos, 4, 24, 32, 35
Nancy Robinson Masters, cover
National Archives, 7, 9, 14, 18, 20, 29, 36, 47
Real War Photos, 22
Larry Sanders, 16, 26, 30

TABLE OF CONTENTS

CHAPTER ONE

World War II Bombing

More than 300 Japanese airplanes attacked Pearl Harbor, Hawaii, on December 7, 1941. The United States had a naval base at Pearl Harbor.

The United States was not expecting the attack. The naval base at Pearl Harbor was not ready to defend itself. The attack killed more than 2,000 people. The Japanese military destroyed almost every ship in Pearl Harbor.

An attack by the Japanese military destroyed Pearl Harbor in 1941.

The bombing brought the United States into World War II (1939-1945). The United States joined a group of countries called the Allied nations. The Allies included Canada, the United Kingdom, France, and Russia. The Allies fought a group of countries called the Axis powers. The Axis powers were Japan, Germany, and Italy.

World War II began in 1939 after Germany invaded Poland. World War II ended in 1945. That was when the United States dropped two atomic bombs on Japan. An atomic bomb is a powerful explosive that destroys large areas. An atomic bomb leaves behind harmful elements after it explodes.

Bombing History

World War II was the first major war in which bombers played a large part. Between 1941 and 1945, the U.S. Army Air Forces (AAF) had 51,221 bombers built. The U.S. Air Force was part of the army during World

World War II was the first major war in which bombers played a large part.

War II. The U.S. Navy and Marines had 27,079 bombers built. Manufacturers built more planes and sent them to other members of the Allied nations.

U.S. bombers dropped more than 3.5 million tons (3.1 million metric tons) of

bombs during World War II. The most
deadly bombs were atomic bombs.

Kinds of Bombers

There were four main kinds of World War II
bombers. Bombers were classed by weight.
The bomber classes were light, medium,
heavy, and very heavy bombers.

Light bombers were the smallest
bombers. Some light bombers like the
Lockheed P-38 Droop Snoot could operate
as fighters or bombers. Fighters were
airplanes designed to protect bombers from
air attacks.

Medium bombers could carry more
bombs than light bombers. But they
could not be used as fighters. Heavy
bombers were the biggest bombers at the
beginning of the war. Heavy bombers could
carry almost twice as many bombs as
medium bombers.

Some light bombers could land on and take off from aircraft carriers.

Very heavy bombers were the largest World War II airplanes. There was only one kind of very heavy bomber in World War II. It was the Boeing B-29 Superfortress. The B-29 could carry twice as many bombs as a heavy bomber.

CHAPTER TWO

Light and Medium Bombers

Light and medium bombers flew short distances and carried light loads. They were cheaper to build than heavier bombers. The Allied nations used medium and light bombers on every front of World War II. A front is a place where militaries are fighting.

Some light bombers could serve as fighters. Light bombers that could serve as fighters or as bombers were called fighter-bombers. In most cases, only one pilot flew a fighter-bomber.

Some light bombers like the A-26 could serve as fighters.

The pilot was also the person who released the bombs.

Medium and light bombers could fly as low as 200 feet (61 meters) above a target. A target is the object at which pilots aim their bombs. Medium and light bombers bombed power stations, roads, and bridges.

North American B-25 Mitchell

The Allies used the North American B-25 Mitchell over Europe. The Mitchell also bombed Japanese ships on the Pacific Ocean. It was the first U.S. aircraft to bomb Japan. Manufacturers built more than 10,000 B-25 Mitchells during World War II.

The Mitchell carried up to 5,000 pounds (2,250 kilograms) of bombs. It could drop bombs from very low altitudes. Altitude is the height of an object above the ground. The Mitchell could drop bombs from altitudes as low as 200 feet (61 meters).

MAJOR PACIFIC AIR BATTLES OF WORLD WAR II

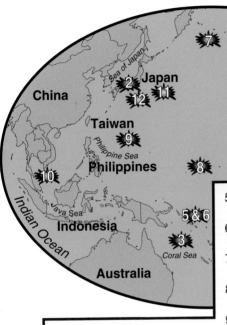

5. Guadalcanal Campaign,
   Aug., 1942 - Feb., 1943
6. Solomon Islands Campaign,
   Feb., 1943 - Nov.,1944
7. Battle of the Komandorski Islands,
   March 26, 1943
8. Truk Attack,
   Feb. 17-18, 1944
9. Battle of the Philippine Sea,
   June 19-20, 1944
10. Battle of Leyte Gulf,
    Oct. 23 - 26, 1944
11. Battle for Iwo Jima
    February, 1945
12. Atomic Bomb dropped on Hiroshima
    August 6, 1945

1. Pearl Harbor,
   Dec. 7,1941
2. Doolittle Raid
   April 18,1942
3. Battle of the Coral Sea,
   May 4-8, 1942
4. Battle of Midway,
   June 3-6, 1942

The B-26 Marauder had the nickname Widow Maker.

Martin B-26 Marauder

The Martin B-26 Marauder had the nickname Widow Maker. Many pilots did not want to fly the Marauder. It was more difficult to fly than many other bombers. Pilots needed extra training to fly it. The Marauder was one of the best medium bombers when flown by trained pilots.

Marauders carried up to 3,000 pounds (1,350 kilograms) of bombs. They dropped bombs from medium altitudes. They could drop bombs accurately from up to 15,000 feet (4,560 meters). Dropping bombs from high altitudes was safer than dropping bombs from low altitudes. Bombers that flew close to the ground were easier for enemies to shoot down.

Lockheed P-38 Droop Snoot

Lockheed built the P-38 Droop Snoot in 1944. Lockheed based it on the P-38 Lightning. The Lightning was one of the earliest successful U.S. fighter airplanes.

The Droop Snoot was a fighter-bomber. It carried up to 4,000 pounds (1,800 kilograms) of bombs. It weighed almost 22,000 pounds (9,900 kilograms).

CHAPTER THREE

Heavy Bombers

The Boeing B-17 Flying Fortress and the Consolidated B-24 Liberator were heavy bombers. They were the most common American heavy bombers in World War II. These bombers carried about twice as many bombs as medium bombers. They bombed from high altitudes.

Boeing B-17 Flying Fortress

The B-17 Flying Fortress was the most famous heavy bomber in World War II. Pilots called it the Flying Fortress because it was hard to destroy. The B-17's wings were 104 feet (31

The B-17 was the most famous heavy bomber of World War II.

The B-17 was known as the airplane that never turned back.

meters) long. It carried up to 6,000 pounds (2,700 kilograms) of bombs. It held a crew of up to 10 people. A B-17's crew always included a pilot, a navigator, and a bombardier. Navigators map courses for pilots to fly. Bombardiers control where and when bombs drop from airplanes.

The first B-17 missions were not successful. A mission is a military task. Pilots from Great Britain tried to use the B-17 at very high altitudes. Air is colder at high altitudes. The B-17s' machine guns froze. The bombs froze in the

18

bomb bays. A bomb bay is the place in an airplane that holds bombs.

The B-17 was almost unstoppable at low altitudes. It could take heavy enemy fire and keep flying. The B-17 was known as the airplane that never turned back.

Consolidated B-24 Liberator

The Consolidated B-24 Liberator was faster than the B-17 Flying Fortress. It could also carry more bombs and travel farther. But the B-24 was not as sturdy as the B-17. It had lighter armor and could not take as much enemy fire. Manufacturers built more than 18,000 B-24s by the end of World War II. That was more than any other World War II airplane.

A B-24 Liberator carried up to 8,800 pounds (3,960 kilograms) of bombs. It had a range of 2,200 miles (3,540 kilometers). The B-24 carried a crew of 10 people. It was armed with 10 machine guns.

The B-24 Liberator served on every front in World War II. Almost every Allied nation flew B-24s. The Allies also used B-24s to carry war supplies.

CHAPTER FOUR

The B-29 Superfortress

There was only one kind of very heavy bomber in World War II. It was the Boeing B-29 Superfortress. A B-29 loaded with bombs weighed 135,000 pounds (61,240 kilograms).

The B-29 needed a crew of at least 10 people. Four to five people operated the B-29's guns. The B-29 had two gun turrets on top, two on the bottom, and one in the tail. A gun turret is a mounting device for guns. Turrets help

The B-29 was the only very heavy bomber of World War II.

A Bomber Crew

1) Bombardier
2) Pilot
3) Copilot
4) Flight Engineer
5) Navigator
6) Radio Operator
7) Top Gunner
8) Left Gunner
9) Right Gunner
10) Radar Observer
11) Tail Gunner

gunners move guns in all directions. The B-29 could carry 20,000 pounds (9,000 kilograms) of bombs.

The Biggest Bomber

The United States built the B-29 Superfortress to increase bombing against Japan. It was bigger, stronger, and flew farther than any bomber before it. Some people called it a superbomber.

The B-29 had 141-foot (43-meter) wings. It had four powerful engines. It could fly at altitudes up to about 38,000 feet (11,500 meters). The B-29 was also the first airplane to use computers. Computers helped gunners control gun turrets.

Bombing Japan

By 1945, about 500 B-29 Superfortresses were bombing Japan. They dropped their bombs from high altitudes. The B-29s flew so high that the Japanese military could not shoot them down easily.

On March 9, 1945, a group of 279 B-29 Superfortresses bombed Tokyo, Japan. The B-29s dropped bombs from 7,000 feet (2,133 meters). Much of Tokyo was burned. The United States hoped the bombing would cause the Japanese to give up. But the Japanese kept fighting.

The *Enola Gay* dropped the first atomic bomb.

The Atomic Bomb

U.S. scientists built the world's first atomic bombs during World War II. The atomic bomb was far more powerful than any bomb built before.

In August 1945, the U.S. military told Japan to surrender. Surrender means to give up a fight or a battle. The United States said Japan would be destroyed if it kept fighting. But the Japanese military was not ready to give up. It did not believe the United States' warning.

On August 6, 1945, the United States sent three B-29s over Japan. Two of the planes carried regular bombs. The other plane carried an atomic bomb. That plane was the *Enola Gay*. A crew member named it after his mother.

The *Enola Gay* carried just one atomic bomb. The military called the bomb Little Boy. It weighed 9,000 pounds. The *Enola Gay* dropped Little Boy on the city of Hiroshima. Three days later, the United States dropped another atomic bomb on Nagasaki, Japan. The Japanese military surrendered. This helped end World War II.

CHAPTER FIVE

Navy and Marine Bombers

Before World War II, the U.S. Navy and Marines had few bombers. The bombers they had were small. Most took off from and landed on aircraft carriers. Aircraft carriers are large warships that carry airplanes.

There were three kinds of U.S. Navy and Marine bombers. They were torpedo bombers, dive bombers, and patrol bombers. Manufacturers built more than 27,000 bombers for the U.S. Navy and Marines during World War II.

This SB2C Helldiver was a navy dive bomber.

Torpedo Bombers

Torpedo bombers aimed at targets on or in water. A torpedo is an explosive that travels underwater. The U.S. Navy and Marines had only one kind of torpedo bomber when World War II began. It was the Douglas TBD Devastator. The Devastator was slow. It carried one 1,000-pound (45-kilogram) torpedo.

In 1941, the United States built a new torpedo bomber. It was the Grumman TBF Avenger. The Avenger could carry 2,000 pounds of bombs. It was sturdier and faster than the Devastator.

The Avenger weighed 18,250 pounds (8,212 kilograms). It was the largest carrier-based airplane in World War II. Carrier-based airplanes take off from and land on aircraft carriers.

Dive Bombers

Dive bombers spotted targets from as high as 12,000 feet (3,657 meters). Then they dove to about 2,000 feet (about 600 meters) and released their bombs.

The TBF Avenger was the largest carrier-based aircraft of World War II.

The Douglas SBD-3 Dauntless dive bomber was slower than most navy planes. It could fly only 250 miles (406 kilometers) per hour. Pilots called it the Slow But Deadly. The Dauntless sank more Japanese ships than any other Allied aircraft. Manufacturers made almost 6,000 Dauntless bombers.

The SB2C Helldiver was larger than the Dauntless. Marine pilots called it the Beast. The Helldiver could fold its wings up. That way it did not take up much space on aircraft carriers.

Patrol Bombers

Patrol bombers searched for and bombed enemy submarines. A submarine is a warship that can run on water or underwater.

The Lockheed PV-1 Ventura was a land-based patrol bomber. It had six machine guns. It could carry 3,000 pounds (1,350 kilograms) of bombs. It also had radar built into its nose. Radar is machinery that sends out radio waves to locate objects. Venturas often flew night missions. Their radar told pilots when enemy airplanes were near.

The Martin PBM Mariner was another patrol bomber. It weighed 60,000 pounds (27,000 kilograms) when loaded with bombs. It could take off and land on water.

The Consolidated PB4Y Privateer was the navy model of the B-24 Liberator. The Privateer could carry 8,800 pounds (3,960 kilograms) of bombs.

The SB2C Helldiver could fold its wings.

CHAPTER SIX

Axis Bombers

The Axis Powers also had bombers during World War II. Axis bombers bombed Allied airfields. They also bombed railroads, bridges, and other important locations. German and Japanese manufacturers built most Axis bombers.

Junkers Ju-87 Stuka

The most famous World War II dive bomber was the German Junkers Ju-87 Stuka. Stuka is a shortened German word for dive bomber.

Many Ju-87 Stukas had loud sirens that screamed as the planes dove. The German air force used the sirens to frighten enemies.

The Stuka was a famous German dive bomber.

The Ju-87 Stuka was not well armed. The German air force used it mainly to attack countries without strong air forces. It could not defeat larger, faster Allied fighters. Germany stopped making Stukas in 1944.

German Heinkel He 111

The German military secretly tested the Heinkel He 111 bomber before World War II. The He 111 weighed more than 30,000 pounds (13,500 kilograms) when it was loaded with bombs. Its wings were more than 74 feet (22 meters) long.

The German military armed the first He 111s with only three machine guns. Allies shot down many He 111s during battles early in the war. Later models of the airplane had more guns. Germany also used He 111s to carry supplies.

Japanese Betty and Peggy

The Mitsubishi G4M was the most famous Japanese bomber. Allies called the G4M the Betty. It was a two-engine bomber. The Betty

Allies shot down many He 111s during battles early in World War II.

could fly 2,000 miles (3,200 kilometers) with a full bomb load.

The Betty was an easy target for U.S. fighters. It carried few guns. Late in the war, Japan added more guns to the Betty.

Allied pilots called the Japanese Ki-67 Hiryus the Peggy. It was Japan's most successful bomber. The Ki-67 could perform loops and turn as quickly as some fast fighter airplanes.

CHAPTER SEVEN

After the War

The U.S. military had a surplus of bombers after World War II. Surplus means more than is needed. The military sent many surplus bombers to airplane graveyards. An airplane graveyard is a place for old and unneeded planes. A few bombers remained in service. The military used them until they became too old.

Surplus Airplanes
The military gave some surplus bombers to other countries' air forces. The military took most bombers apart and melted them in smelters. A smelter is a furnace where metal is melted.

The military sent many surplus dive bombers to airplane graveyards.

Some World War II bombers are still flying today.

Manufacturers reused metal from the bombers to make window screens and other items for construction. The United States sent many of these items to Germany, Italy, and Japan. The metal helped these countries rebuild after World War II.

Still Flying
Some World War II bombers are still flying today. Museums and collectors restore them. Restore means to bring back to original condition.

Some people build restored airplanes with pieces from many airplanes. They get some of the pieces from airplane graveyards. The Flying Tigers Warbird Restoration Museum rebuilds World War II planes. The museum has rebuilt bombers such as the B-17. Members of the American Airpower Heritage Museum rebuilt a B-29. It is the only B-29 flying today.

Museums

Most World War II bombers cannot fly anymore. Some of them are in museums.

The National Museum of Naval Aviation has more than 150 airplanes. The museum has a PB4Y Privateer and an SBD Dauntless. It also has an SB2C Helldiver.

The National Air and Space Museum in Washington, D.C., also displays World War II aircraft. The museum's most famous display is the *Enola Gay*. The museum does not display the whole airplane. It is too big. The museum displays the *Enola Gay's* cockpit, engines, and bomb bay. The display gives visitors a chance to see an important piece of world history.

tail

gun turret

A-26 Invader fighter-bomber

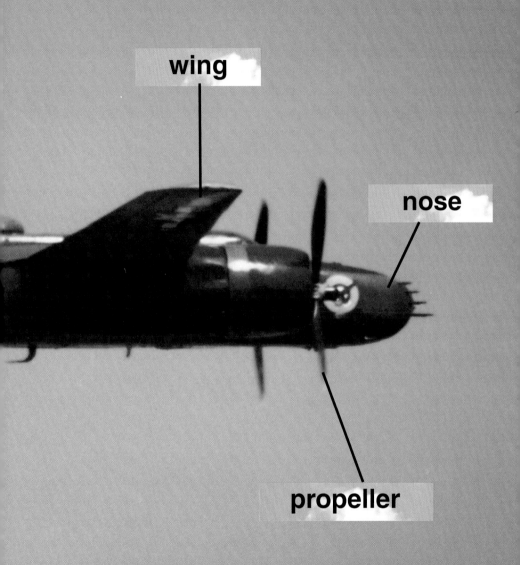

wing

nose

propeller

WORDS TO KNOW

aircraft carrier (AIR-kraft KAIR-ee-ur)—a large warship that carries airplanes

altitude (AL-ti-tood)—the height of an object above the ground

atomic bomb (uh-TOM-ik BOM)—a powerful explosive that destroys large areas; it leaves behind harmful elements after it explodes.

bombardier (bom-buh-DIHR)—a bombing crew member who controls where and when bombs drop from airplanes

bomb bay (BOM BAY)—the place on an airplane that holds bombs

front (FRUHNT)—a place where militaries are fighting.

gun turret (GUHN TUR-it)— a mounting device for guns

mission (MISH-uhn)—a military task

navigator (NAV-uh-gay-tuhr)—a bombing crew member who maps a course for the pilot to fly

radar (RAY-dar)—machinery that uses radio waves to locate objects

restore (ri-STOR)—to bring back to original condition

smelter (SMELT-er)—a furnace where metal is melted

submarine (SUHB-muh-reen)— a warship that can travel on top of the water and underwater

surplus (SUR-pluhss)—more than is needed

surrender (suh-REN-dur)—to give up a fight or battle

target (TAR-git)—the object at which pilots aim their bombs

torpedo (tor-PEE-doh)—an explosive that travels underwater

TO LEARN MORE

Baines, Francesca. *Planes*. New York: Franklin Watts, 1995.

Masters, Nancy Robinson. *Airplanes of World War II*. Mankato, Minn.: Capstone High/Low Books, 1998.

Masters, Nancy Robinson. *Training Planes of World War II*. Mankato, Minn.: Capstone High/Low Books, 1998.

Schleifer, Jay. *Bomber Planes*. Minneapolis: Capstone Press, 1996.

USEFUL ADDRESSES

American Airpower Heritage Museum
P. O. Box 62000
Midland, Texas 79711

National Air and Space Museum
Seventh Street and Independence Avenue
Washington, DC 20560

National Aviation Museum
P. O. Box 9724
Ottawa, Ontario KIG 543
Canada

United States Air Force Museum
Wright-Patterson Air Force Base
Dayton, OH 45433

INTERNET SITES

Enola Gay
http://www.nasm.edu/GALLERIES/GAL103/
  gal103.html

Military Aircraft Database
http://www.csd.uwo.ca/~pettypi/elevon/gustin_
  military/

Welcome to the National Warplane Museum
http://www.warplane.org/warplanes.html

WWII Airplanes
http://canopus.lpi.msk.su/~watson/wwiiap.html

INDEX